# Inside My Body

# Why do I burp?

Isabel Thomas

**www.raintreepublishers.co.uk**
Visit our website to find out
more information about
Raintree books.

**To order:**
☎ Phone 0845 6044371
▤ Fax +44 (0) 1865 312263
▣ Email myorders@raintreepublishers.co.uk

Customers from outside the UK please telephone +44 1865 312262

Raintree is an imprint of Capstone Global Library Limited,
a company incorporated in England and Wales having its
registered office at 7 Pilgrim Street, London, EC4V 6LB –
Registered company number: 6695582

Text © Capstone Global Library Limited 2011
First published in hardback in 2011
The moral rights of the proprietor have been asserted.

Edited by Kate de Villiers and Laura Knowles
Designed by Steve Mead
Illustrations by KJA-artists.com
Picture research by Mica Brancic
Originated by Capstone Global Library Ltd
Printed and bound in China by CTPS

ISBN 978 1 406 22102 2 (hardback)
15 14 13 12 11
10 9 8 7 6 5 4 3 2 1

**British Library Cataloguing in Publication Data**
Thomas, Isabel, 1980-
Why do I burp?. -- (Inside my body)
612.3-dc22
A full catalogue record for this book is available from the
British Library.

**Acknowledgements**
We would like to thank the following for permission
to reproduce photographs: © Capstone Publishers
p. **7** (Karon Dubke); Corbis p. **25** (© Paul Souders);
Getty Images p. **5** (Photonica/White Packert); Getty
Images News pp. **13** (isifa/Libor Fojtik), **26** (Jasper
Juinen); NASA p. **27**; Photolibrary p. **10** (Juniors
Bildarchiv); Science Photo Library pp. **14** (Eye of
Science), **17** (Susumu Nishinaga), **18** (Eye of Science),
**21** (Scimat), **22** (Scimat), **9** (3445128471); Shutterstock
pp. **15** (Eric Gevaert), **23** (Sascha Burkard).

Photographic design details reproduced with permission
of Shutterstock pp. **4**, **19**, **22** (© Isaac Marzioli), **4**, **19**,
**22** (© Yurok).

Cover photograph of girl with hand over mouth
reproduced with permission of Corbis/Retna Ltd./
© Rena Durham.

We would like to thank David Wright for his invaluable
help in the preparation of this book.

# Contents

Words that appear in the text in bold, **like this**, are explained in the glossary on page 30.

# Why do I burp?

You're finishing off a meal when you feel something bubbling up from deep inside. Your hand clamps over your mouth just in time. BURRRRP!

When you eat and drink, you swallow small bubbles of air. This air gets trapped in your **digestive system** (the rollercoaster of tubes that food travels through after you eat). The air is squeezed as you eat and drink more. Finally the trapped air escapes, making a loud noise on its way out.

Air is not the only **gas** that gets trapped in your digestive system. Other gases are formed as food travels through your body. Trapped gases that can't escape through your mouth travel through your whole digestive system and exit from your bottom!

## Practical advice

### Blame it on the food

Burping three to four times after a meal is normal. You might burp more if you eat too quickly or drink through a straw, as you will swallow extra air.

Getting these trapped gases out of the way is handy, because your digestive system has an important job to do. It breaks food down so your body can use all the good stuff locked inside. This process is called digestion.

Fizzy drinks can cause big burps, because they contain extra gas. The little bubbles of a gas called carbon dioxide gather in your tummy before bursting back out.

# Why is digestion important?

Food needs to be broken down before your body can use it for energy and growth. The useful substances in food are called **nutrients**. Each type of nutrient does a different job in your body.

Your **digestive system** has to break down chunks of food into **particles** of carbohydrate, fat, and protein that are tiny enough to travel in and out of **cells** and zoom around in your blood.

**Your digestive system is made of several different zones. Throughout the book, this diagram will help you to discover what your food faces in each zone.**

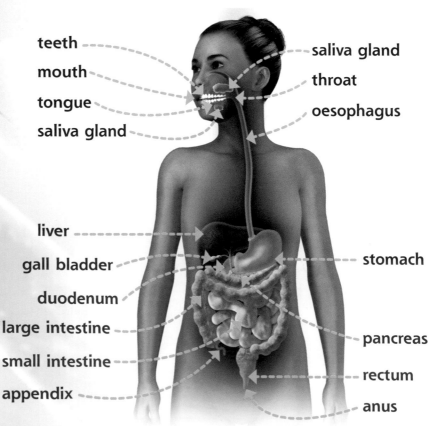

teeth
mouth
tongue
saliva gland

saliva gland
throat
oesophagus

liver
gall bladder
duodenum
large intestine
small intestine
appendix

stomach
pancreas
rectum
anus

This book will take you on a tour around the digestive system. Climb on board the digestive rollercoaster to find out how your body breaks down food to get at the nutrients inside. Watch out for the things that make you burp!

🔍 **The nutrients found in foods are the building materials for cells. You couldn't live without them.**

Foods such as bread and pasta contain sugars and starches (also called carbohydrates). They provide instant energy. Your body uses energy all the time, even as you sleep.

All foods contain **vitamins** and **minerals**. These do special jobs that keep your body healthy.

Fruit and vegetables contain a lot of water. Your food provides a fifth of the water you need each day.

Meat, fish, eggs, and beans contain proteins. Proteins carry out complicated tasks such as carrying messages around your body, killing germs, and building muscles. Special proteins called **enzymes** even help to digest food.

Milk, cheese, and butter contain fats. Fats keep your body warm and cushion your organs from bumps and bangs. They also release energy slowly, so your body keeps working even if you haven't eaten for a while.

# How does digestion start?

Seeing, smelling, and even thinking about food kicks your **digestive system** into action. Saliva glands squirt saliva (spit) into your mouth, ready for the first bite.

Teeth are specially shaped to help break food down. After your front teeth bite off a chewable chunk, your tongue pushes the food around your mouth. The flat-topped back teeth crush and grind it into smaller pieces.

teeth

mouth

tongue

saliva glands

throat

**DIGESTION ZONE: mouth**
**TIME: 20 seconds**
**WATCH OUT FOR: biting and grinding teeth, saliva**

## What does the tongue do?

Your tongue is covered with tiny bumps that send information about food to your brain. Some are spiky, gripping and moving food as you chew. Other bumps detect whether food is hot or cold, rough or smooth.

The bumps are also home to up to 8,000 taste buds that tell you if food is sweet, sour, salty, bitter, or **umami**. Along with sight and smell, taste tells your body if food is safe to eat.

Eating the same thing every day would be unhealthy – and boring! Our sense of taste means that we enjoy a range of foods.

# What does my saliva do?

So far your food hasn't had much fun. It has been pushed by your tongue, crushed by your teeth, and soaked in slimy saliva.

🔍 **Digestive enzymes are very powerful. Tarantulas don't need to chew – instead, they inject saliva into their prey. Enzymes in the saliva dissolve the victim's insides, turning it into a soup, which the tarantula sucks up.**

Saliva is also packed with proteins called **enzymes**. These help your body to break food down more quickly. Enzymes grab on to chemicals in the food and split them into **particles** too tiny to see.

## A sweet taste

Different enzymes attack food as it travels through your **digestive system**. Each one breaks down a certain type of food. The enzyme in saliva begins to digest starch, turning it into tiny particles of sugar. As the sugar washes over your tongue, food starts tasting sweeter.

Chewing mixes your food with saliva, making it softer. The **mucus** in saliva gives food a slimy coating so it can be easily swallowed. Your tongue pushes a bolus (ball) of soft food to the back of your throat. A long tube called the **oesophagus** leads the way to your stomach.

## SCIENCE BEHIND THE MYTH

**MYTH:** The only cause of bad breath is not brushing your teeth.

**SCIENCE:** Brushing your teeth is important, but did you know that a dry mouth can also cause bad breath? Saliva freshens your mouth by killing bacteria that build up on your teeth. Keep it topped up by drinking plenty of water.

# What makes a burp so noisy?

Your **oesophagus** moves food from your mouth to your stomach. Food doesn't just fall down the pipe. Muscles in the oesophagus walls squeeze together and push the ball of food towards your stomach. It's a bit like pushing toothpaste out of a tube!

This swallowing action even works if you stand on your head. Food is moved through your whole **digestive system** in the same way.

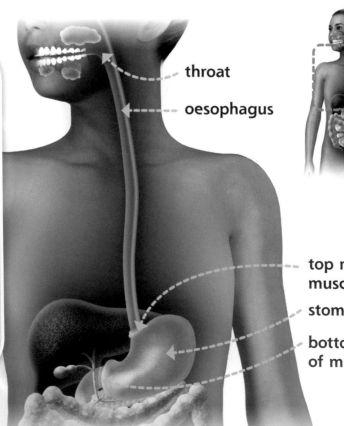

throat

oesophagus

top ring of muscle

stomach

bottom ring of muscle

P Your stomach can hold about a litre of chewed food. These competitive eaters' stomachs stretch like balloons as they are filled with food.

## Extreme body fact

### Record-breaking burp
Paul Hunn produced the world's loudest burp in 2008. His 107-decibel belch would damage your hearing if you stood too close. Paul did it by contracting his abdominal muscles to force gas out quickly.

## The muscle to blame

At the bottom of the oesophagus, a ring of muscle opens to let food into your stomach. It closes again to seal the food inside. You can blame this muscle for noisy burps. When trapped **gas** escapes from your stomach, it bursts through the ring of muscle. The muscle vibrates (moves from side to side) like the neck of a balloon when air escapes. The vibrations make a noise.

Air might be able to escape from your stomach, but your food is not so lucky. Read on to find out what it faces next.

# What happens inside my stomach?

Your stomach has two jobs. Super-stretchy walls let it store big meals, so your body can digest the food slowly. Your stomach also kick-starts digestion by mixing food with **gastric juices**.

The walls of your stomach are covered in gastric pits, which squirt food with a sticky combination of **mucus**, acid, and enzymes.

## Gastric juice

Little pits in your stomach's lining pump out around 1.5 litres (2.5 pints) of gastric juice every day. This isn't the kind of juice that you'd want to drink. It contains **enzymes** and a strong acid. The enzymes start to digest proteins. The acid kills nasty germs that may have hitched a ride on your food. It also helps the protein-chomping enzymes to work.

Strong muscles in the stomach walls toss everything around like a cement mixer. This turns your lovely meal into a sloppy paste. If you've ever been sick, you'll know exactly what this paste looks like! There is a ring of muscle at the bottom of your stomach. It opens to let the paste squirt through, a little at a time.

### Extreme body fact

**Burping is not green**
Cows are the world's biggest burpers. They burp methane **gas**, which is formed as grass is digested in their four stomachs. Methane is one of the gases that cause global warming. There are so many cattle farms that cow burps release more global warming gas than the world's planes, trains, and cars!

# What happens in my small intestine?

The small intestine is a long, narrow tube coiled up beneath your stomach. It is here that your body finishes digesting and then **absorbs** (takes in) the **nutrients** in food.

The duodenum is the first part of the small intestine. Here the food is drenched in digestive juices from the **pancreas**, and bombarded by bile from the gall bladder. These juices continue breaking down fats, proteins, carbohydrates, **vitamins**, and **minerals** into tiny **particles**.

liver     duodenum     bottom ring of muscle     small intestine

gall bladder

pancreas

**DIGESTION ZONE:** small intestine, gall bladder, and pancreas

**LENGTH:** 6-7 metres (20-30 feet)

**TIME:** up to 4 hours

**WATCH OUT FOR:** fat-busting bile

## Super enzymes

**Enzymes** are the intestine's secret weapons. As food passes into the small intestine, extra enzymes squirt out from glands in the intestine walls, along with water and **mucus**.

Bile is a green digestive juice made by the liver. It is stored in the gall bladder until the body needs it. Bile breaks fats down into tiny droplets, like washing up liquid dissolving pan grease. Enzymes can lock on to these droplets to break them down further. The thin, watery food mixture is now full of food particles small enough to pass through the intestine wall.

The intestine walls are criss-crossed with blood vessels that are ready to absorb all the nutrients from the digested food.

### Extreme body fact

Your **digestive system** breaks food down into particles that are 10 million times smaller than a lump of swallowed food. This is the same as breaking Mount Everest down into grains of sand.

# How does food get into my blood?

The "small" intestine is actually the longest part of your **digestive system**. It provides plenty of space for your body to **absorb** all the **nutrients** in food.

The intestine lining is not smooth. It is covered with millions of tiny "tentacles" called villi. These tentacles increase the **surface area**, so there is even more space.

🔍 **This is a magnified image of villi. These tiny parts give the small intestine a surface area as big as a tennis court.**

Most types of food **particle**, as well as water and **minerals**, are absorbed through the small intestine wall and into the blood vessels that surround it.

Once nutrients are in the bloodstream, their first stop is the liver. This huge organ sorts out the nutrients so that your body is not flooded with food after a meal. Some nutrients are stored. Others are put back in the blood and sent around the body. Harmful substances are removed. The **pancreas** helps out by making a substance that controls the amount of sugar in your blood.

## Practical advice

### How do I know when I'm full?

As you eat, your digestive system sends signals to your brain, making you feel full. This is your body's way of telling you to stop eating. It can take 15 to 20 minutes after food is first eaten for all these signals to get to the brain. If you eat too quickly, force yourself to finish large portions, or choose too many foods high in fat and sugar, you may take in more food than you need.

# What happens to food my body can't use?

Not everything that you eat can be digested. **Enzymes** can't break down many substances found in plants. These substances are known as fibre.

The leftover material moves into the large intestine (shorter but fatter than the small intestine). Your body is careful not to waste anything useful. Water, salts, and some **vitamins** are **absorbed**.

**DIGESTION ZONE:** large intestine and rectum
**LENGTH:** 1.5 metres (5 feet)   **TIME:** 1 to 3 days
**DIAMETER:** 7 to 10 cm   **WATCH OUT FOR:** billions of bacteria

large intestine

colon

appendix

rectum

anus

🔍 Billions of bacteria live in your digestive system, and make up almost a third of your poo. They are known as "friendly" bacteria because they help your body to break down food.

## Poo!

As water is drawn out, the leftover material gets harder. It is now solid **faeces** (poo). It contains substances that your body wants to get rid of, such as used-up red blood **cells**. These are passed into the intestine from the liver and give faeces a brown colour, no matter what you've been eating.

The faeces are gradually pushed into the rectum. They are stored here until they have a chance to exit the body by being pushed through the anus, a ring of muscle at the bottom of the **digestive system**. This might happen the next time you visit the loo!

### Extreme body fact

**Bottom burps**
If swallowed air is not burped up, it is passed as wind. Most people pass wind (fart) between 6 and 20 times a day.

# What happens if I eat something bad?

Germs such as bacteria love food. When bacteria find themselves on a plate of food at the right temperature and surrounded by plenty of air, they quickly grow in numbers.

## Keep your food germ-free

✔ Don't sneeze and cough over food

✔ Wash your hands before cooking or eating

✔ Cook and reheat food properly – heat kills bacteria

✔ Keep raw food away from cooked food

✔ Store food in air-tight containers

✔ Keep food cool. Bacteria grow more slowly in a fridge or freezer.

🔍 Bacteria can only be seen with a microscope. These *E. coli* bacteria live on some foods and can cause food poisoning.

## Food poisoning

Eating food that has germs on it can make you ill with food poisoning. Your **digestive system** reacts by squeezing food and water out of each end. This vomiting and diarrhoea helps your body to get rid of the dangerous food quickly.

Vomiting starts when germs irritate your stomach lining. Sensors send messages to your brain, which tells your **diaphragm** to contract. The ring of muscle at the top of your stomach opens, and a big push forces food up your **oesophagus** and out of your mouth. Yuck!

Being sick is very unpleasant. The **gastric juice** from your stomach makes vomit very acidic. It can burn your throat.

🔍 **Houseflies don't mind being sick. A fly vomits digestive juices on to food before sucking the softened snack back up. This spreads germs very easily – the fly's last meal may have been a steaming pile of poo.**

# How can I take care of my digestive system?

Your **digestive system** works hard to keep the good bits from food and to get rid of the bad bits. Like any machine, it works better if you take care of it. Indigestion, bloating, burping, and hiccups are all signs that your digestive system might need a service.

Eating slowly and chewing food helps your stomach to cope with big meals. Eating too quickly can irritate your stomach and **oesophagus**, and might also cause hiccups.

## Extreme body fact

### Hiccups for life

When you hiccup, your **diaphragm** contracts quickly, sucking in air. The "hic" is the sound of the flap that separates your air and food tubes snapping shut. American Charles Osborne had the world's longest case of hiccups – from 1922 until 1990!

## A healthy diet

You can keep your digestive system working smoothly by eating a healthy diet that includes fibre. You can't digest fibre, so it gives the muscles of your digestive system something to push on as they move food through your body. Bulky fibre also helps you to feel full for longer.

Your body is nearly two-thirds water. Drinking six to eight glasses of water a day keeps it topped up. Fibre **absorbs** some of this water, which makes leftover material bulkier.

High-fat foods are difficult for your digestive system to break down. Taking a break from fatty foods helps food to move through your digestive system more quickly.

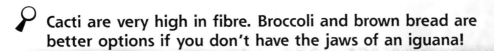 Cacti are very high in fibre. Broccoli and brown bread are better options if you don't have the jaws of an iguana!

# How long does digestion take?

On the digestive rollercoaster your food is attacked by acids, bathed in bile, and ambushed by **enzymes**. Fats, proteins, and carbohydrates are broken down and taken up by your blood. The bits your body doesn't fancy are sucked dry and squeezed out. It's enough to make you burp.

Spain's La Tomatina festival is the world's biggest food fight. About 140 tonnes of tomatoes are broken up without any help from the **digestive system!**

Eating in space can be tricky. An astronaut's digestive system has to work hard too.

In just six to eight hours, a meal is transformed into a collection of **nutrients** whizzing around in your bloodstream and helping your body to grow, study, play, and digest the next meal. That's right – it's time to do it all over again.

# Your amazing digestion

Burping a lot is one sign of indigestion. Watch out for these burp hazards to keep your **digestive system** working smoothly:

Drinking through a straw

Swallowing bubbles of air as you eat normally

Eating too quickly

**Gases** forming in stomach as food is broken down

Drinking fizzy drinks

## Top ten BURP HAZARDS!

Stomach too full from overeating

Exercising too soon after eating

Stomach acid escaping into the **oesophagus**

Lying down too soon after eating

Indigestion from eating too many fatty foods

# The digestive system

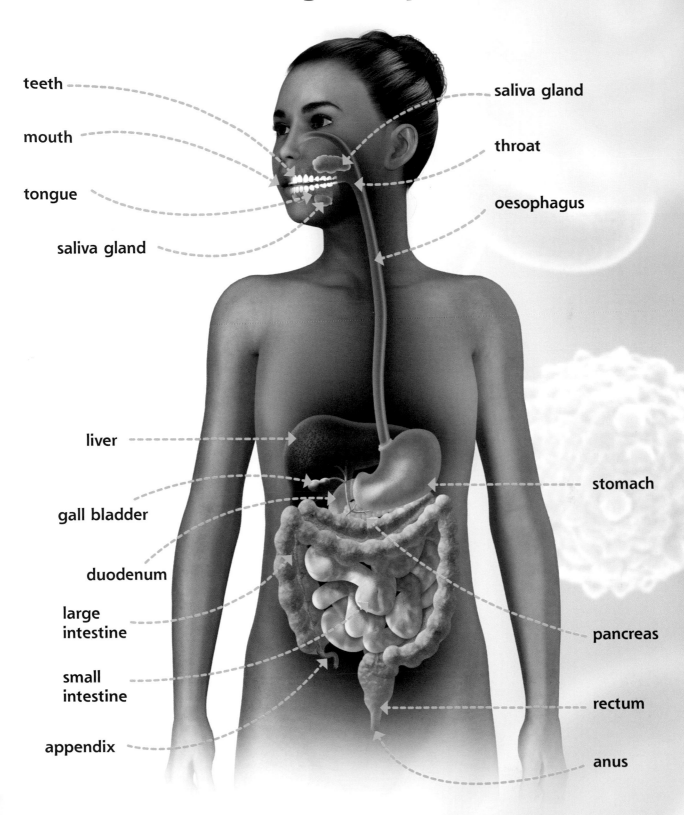

teeth

mouth

tongue

saliva gland

saliva gland

throat

oesophagus

liver

gall bladder

duodenum

large intestine

small intestine

appendix

stomach

pancreas

rectum

anus

# Glossary

**absorb** take in

**cell** smallest part of a living thing

**diaphragm** large muscle that sits between your lungs and your digestive system, and controls breathing

**digestive system** all the organs that help your body to digest and absorb food, and to get rid of undigested food

**enzyme** special protein that helps your body to break down food into small particles

**faeces** (poo) solid waste that leaves your digestive system

**gas** substance that is not liquid or solid, and can move about like air. Oxygen and methane are types of gas.

**gastric juice** fluid released from glands in the stomach lining, containing enzymes and acid to help digest food

**gravity** force that pulls everything downwards towards Earth

**mineral** natural substance not made by living things. Your body needs minerals to help it grow, develop, and function.

**mucus** thick, slippery substance that helps your food to pass smoothly through the digestive system

**nutrient** substance that your body needs to grow, develop, and function

**oesophagus** tube linking your mouth to your stomach

**pancreas** organ near your stomach that makes digestive juices to help your body break down food, and a substance to control blood sugar levels

**particle** extremely small piece of something

**surface area** outside of something; the part that is in contact with other substances

**umami** type of savoury taste in foods such as meat and fish

**vitamin** natural substance made by living things. Your body needs vitamins to help it grow, develop, and function.

# Find out more

## Books

*The Digestive System (Body Systems)*, Sue Barraclough
    (Heinemann Library, 2008)
*First Human Body Encyclopedia*, Penny Smith
    (Dorling Kindersley, 2005)

## Websites

**www.foodafactoflife.org.uk**
The British Nutrition Foundation's website has interactive games to find out about eating well and keeping your digestive system healthy.

**www.childrenfirst.nhs.uk/kids/health/eat_smart/poo_corner**
Visit this web page to find out about all the different kinds of poo. Yuck!

**yucky.discovery.com/flash/body/pg000029.html**
Select "Belches and gas" on this website to find all the yuckiest facts about how your body breaks down food. The site contains sound effects and animations.

## A place to visit

Science Museum
Exhibition Road, London SW7 2DD
www.sciencemuseum.org.uk
The Science Museum often has exhibits and special events for children about digestion.

# Index